THE SMIT

"STRANGEWAYS, HERE WE COME"

Music Transcribed by Phil Davies
Music Processed by Musicprint Ltd
Photographs by Jo Novark
Designed and Printed by Panda Press

THE SMITHS
"STRANGEWAYS, HERE WE COME"

A RUSH AND A PUSH AND THE LAND IS OURS

HELLO
I am the ghost of Troubled Joe
hung by his pretty white neck
some eighteen months ago
I travelled to a mystical time zone
but I missed my bed
so I soon came home
they said:
"there's too much caffeine
in your blood stream
and a lack of real spice
in your life"
I said:
"leave me alone
because I'm alright, dad
just surprised to still
be on my own...."
Ooh, but don't mention love
I'd hate the strain of the pain again
a rush and a push and the land that
we stand on is ours
it has been before
so it shall be again
and people who are uglier than you and I
they take what they need, and leave
Ooh, but don't mention love
I'd hate the pain of the strain all over again
a rush and a push and the land that
we stand on is ours
it has been before
so why can't it be now?
and people who are weaker than you and I
they take what they want from life
Ooh, but don't mention love
no – just don't mention love!
a rush and a push and the land that
we stand on is ours
your youth may be gone
but you're still a young man
so phone me, phone me, phone me
so phone me, phone me, phone me
Ooh, I think I'm in love
Ooh, I think I'm in love
Ooh, I think I'm in love
Urrgh, I think I'm in lerv

A Rush And A Push And The Land Is Ours

Words by
MORRISSEY

Music by
JOHNNY MARR

B♭ C Dm C B♭ C
and I missed my bed and I soon came home they said "There's
Dm C B♭ C Dm C
too much caf-fine in your blood stream and a lack of re-al spice in your life"
B♭ C Dm C B♭ C
I said leave me a-lone be-cause I'm al-right dad sur-
Dm C B♭ C
prised to still be on my own."

Eb
Dm7
Eb
Ooh but don't men-tion love I'd hate the strain of the pain a - gain
Ooh but don't men-tion love I'd hate the pain of the strain all over again
Ooh but don't men-tion love no no don't men - tion love
Dm7
Bb
C
Dm
C
Bb
C
A rush and a push and the land that we stand on is ours.
Dm
C
Bb
C
Dm
C
it has been be - fore so it shall be a - gain and peo-ple who are
it has been be - fore so it shall be a - gain and peo-ple who are
your youth may be gone but you're still a young man so phone me phone

B♭ C Dm C
1. 2.
B♭ C
ug - li - er than you and I they take what they need and just leave.
weak - er than you and I they take what they want from life.
me so phone me phone me phone
3.
B♭ C E♭ Dm7
me. Ooh I think I'm in love
E♭ Dm7 E♭
ooh I think I'm in love ooh I think I'm in love
Dm7 E♭ Dm7
think I'm in love urrgh I think I'm in love.
etc.

I STARTED SOMETHING I COULDN'T FINISH

The lanes were silent
with nothing or no one around for miles
I doused our friendly venture
with a hard-faced
three-word gesture
I started something
I forced you into a zone
and you were clearly
never meant to go
hair brushed and parted
typical me, typical me
typical me
I started something
. . . and now I'm not too sure
I grabbed you by the guilded beams
that's what Tradition means
and I doused another venture
with a gesture
that was . . . absolutely vile
I started something
I forced you into a zone
and you were clearly
never meant to go
hair brushed and parted
typical me, typical me
typical me
I started something
. . . and now I'm not too sure
I grabbed you by the guilded beams
that's what Tradition means
and now eighteen months' hard-labour
seems . . . fair enough
I started something
I forced you into a zone
and you were clearly
never meant to go
hair brushed and parted
typical me, typical me
typical me
I started something
and now I'm not too sure

I Started Something I Couldn't Finish

Words by
MORRISSEY

Music by
JOHNNY MARR

A
A♯
I
And I
And now
Bm
doused our friend - ly ven - ture with a
doused a no - ther ven - ture with a
eighteen months hard labour seems
D
E
hard faced three - word ges - ture.
ges - ture that was ab - solutely vile.
fair enough.

CHORUS
C#m7
C#7
I start - ed some - thing I forced you in - to a zone
D7
E7
F7
and you were clear - ly ne - ver meant to go.
F#
C#m7
Hair brushed and part - - ed
C#7
ty - pi - cal me ty - pi - cal me ty - pi - cal me I start - ed

D7
E7
F7
1. 3.
F♯
some - thing
and now I'm not too sure.
(to CHORUS – 3º)
A
A♯
2. I
2.
F♯
sure.
A
A♯
3. I

DEATH OF A DISCO DANCER

The death of a disco dancer
well, it happens a lot 'round here
and if you think Peace
is a common goal
well, that goes to show
just how little you know
The death of a disco dancer
well, I'd rather not get involved
I never talk to my neighbour
I'd just rather not get involved
Love, peace and harmony?
Love, peace and harmony?
Oh, very nice
very nice
very nice
very nice
. . . but maybe in the next world

Death Of A Disco Dancer

Words by
MORRISSEY

Music by
JOHNNY MARR

B A G♯m7 G
if you think peace is a com-mon goal that goes to show how lit - tle you know.
talk to my neigh - bour I'd ra - ther not get in - volved.
1. B A G♯m7 E
The
2. B A
G♯m7 E B A G♯m7 G
B A G♯m7 E

B A G♯m7 G
Love peace and har-mo-ny
B A G♯m7 E
love peace and har - mo - ny oh
B A G♯m7 G
ve-ry nice ve-ry nice ve-ry nice ve-ry nice but may-be in the
B A G♯m7 E
next world.
D.𝄋.

GIRLFRIEND IN A COMA

Girlfriend in a coma, I know
I know – it's serious
Girlfriend in a coma, I know
I know – it's really serious
there were times when I could
have 'murdered' her
(but, you know, I would hate
anything to happen to her)
NO, I DON'T WANT TO SEE HER
Do you really think
she'll pull through?
Do you really think
she'll pull through?
Girlfriend in a coma, I know
I know – it's serious
there were times when I could
have 'strangled' her
(but, you know, I would hate
anything to happen to her)
WOULD YOU PLEASE
LET ME SEE HER!
Do you really think
she'll pull through?
Do you really think
she'll pull through?
Let me whisper my last goodbyes

I know – IT'S SERIOUS

Girlfriend In A Coma

Words by
MORRISSEY

Music by
JOHNNY MARR

C D G Gmaj7
There were times when I could have mur - dered her.
There were times when I could have stran - gled her.
C D G Gmaj7 C D
But you know I would hate an - y - thing to hap - pen to her,
But you know I would hate an - y - thing to hap - pen to her,
G Gmaj7 C D
no I don't want to see her.
would you please let me see her.
Do you

Em D C D Em D
real - ly think she'll pull through, do you real - ly think she'll _ pull through _
C Em D
_ ooh. _
1. C D
2. C D
Let me
G Gmaj7 C D G
whis - per my last _ good - byes, _ I know _ it's ser - i - ous. _

45rpm
THE PRIMITIVES
killing

STOP ME IF YOU THINK YOU'VE HEARD THIS ONE BEFORE

Stop me, stop me
stop me if you think that you've
heard this one before
stop me, stop me
stop me if you think that you've
heard this one before
nothing's changed
I still love you, oh I still love you
. . . only slightly less than I used to
I was delayed, I was way-laid
an emergency stop
I smelt the last ten seconds of life
I crashed down on the crossbar
and the pain was enough to make
a shy, bald buddhist reflect
and plan a mass-murder
who said I'd lied to her?
who said I'd lied because I never
who said I'd lied because I never
I was detained, I was restrained
he broke my spleen
he broke my knees
(and then he really laid into me)
Friday night in Out-patients
who said I'd lied to her?
who said I'd lied – because I never
who said I'd lied – because I never
Oh, so I drank one
or was it four
and when I fell on the floor . . .
. . . I drank more
stop me, stop me
stop me if you think that you've
heard this one before
nothing's changed
I still love you
I still love you
but only slightly
less than I used to

Stop Me If You Think You've Heard This One Before

Words by
MORRISSEY

Music by
JOHNNY MARR

Gm7
E♭
F
stop me. Stop me if you think that you've heard this one be - fore
C7
Gm7
E♭
no - thing's changed I still love you oh I still love you
F
To Coda ⊕
C7
Gm7
on - ly slight - ly on - ly slight - ly less than I
E♭
F
G♯maj7(+9)
used to my love.

C♯m7(+9)
G♯maj7(+9)
B♭
G
B♭
C7
Gm7
I was de - layed I was way - laid an e -
I was de - layed I was re - strained he broke my
E♭
F
mer - gen - cy stop I smelt the last ten se - conds of life
spleen he broke me knee and then he real - ly laid in - to me

C7
Gm7
E♭
— I crashed down on the cross - bar and the pain was en-ough to make a
Fri-day night in out pa-tients who said I'd lied to her
F
C7
Gm7
shy bald Bud-dist re-flect — and plan — a mass mur - der who
oh who said I'd lied be-cause I never I never
E♭
F
C7
said I'd lied to her — oh who said I'd lied — be-cause I
who said I'd lied because I never — and so I drank one — it be-came
Gm7
E♭
F
ne-ver I ne-ver who said I'd lied — be-cause I ne-ver.
four and when I fell on the floor I drank more.

G♯maj7(+9)
C♯m7(+9)
G♯maj7(+9)
B♭
1.
G
B♭
2.
G
D.S. al Coda
B♭
CODA
F♯m7
G7
rall.

LAST NIGHT I DREAMT THAT SOMEBODY LOVED ME

Last night I dreamt
that somebody loved me
no hope – but no harm
just another false alarm
Last night I felt
real arms around me
no hope – no harm
just another false alarm
so, tell me how long
before the last one?
and tell me how long
before the right one?
this story is old – I KNOW
but it goes on
this story is old – I KNOW
but it goes on

Last Night I Dreamt That Somebody Loved Me

Words by
MORRISSEY

Music by
JOHNNY MARR

C
B♭/D
C/E
Am/D
Am/C
Gm
B♭/F
Gm
B♭/F
C/E
Em
C
1. Last night I dreamt
2. Last night I felt

Cm
Bm7
B7
that some - bo - dy loved me.
real arms a - round me.
Em
C
no hope no heart just a -
no hope no heart just a -
Cm
1.
Bm7
no - ther false a - larm.
no - ther false a - larm.
B7
2.
Bm7
B7
So tell me how long

Em
C
be - fore the last one
I know but it goes on
Cm
Bm7
B7
and tell me how long
this sto - ry is old
Em
C
be - fore the right one.
I know but it goes on.
Cm
Bm7
B7
This sto - ry is old

45 rpm
PRIMITIVES
killing me

UNHAPPY BIRTHDAY

I've come to wish you an unhappy birthday
I've come to wish you an unhappy birthday
because you're evil
and you lie
and if you should die
I may feel slightly sad
(but I won't cry)
Loved and lost
and some may say
when usually its Nothing
surely you're happy
it should be this way?
I say "No, I'm gonna kill my dog"
and: "May the lines sag heavy
and deep tonight XXX"
I've come to wish you an unhappy birthday
I've come to wish you an unhappy birthday
because you're evil
and you lie
and if you should die
I may feel slightly sad
(But I won't cry)
Loved and lost
some people say
when usually its Nothing
surely you're happy
it should be this way?
I said "No"
and then I shot myself
so, drink, drink, drink
and be ill tonight
from the one you left behind
from the one you left behind
from the one you left behind
from the one you left behind
XXXXXXXXX

Unhappy Birthday

Words by
MORRISSEY

Music by
JOHNNY MARR

B♭6
G
D
day 'cos you're ev - il and you lie and if you should
day 'cos you're ev - il and you lie and if you should
F6
B♭6
G
die I may feel slight - ly sad but I won't
die I may feel slight - ly sad but I won't
D
F6
D
cry.
cry.
G
D
Loved and lost and some may

C6
D
say
when us - ual - ly it's noth - ing sure-
Am7(+4)
Cmaj7(+6)
ly you're hap - py it should be this way.
I say
I said
D
"no I'm gon na kill my dog"
"no" and then I shot my - self
D
"may the lines sag the lines sag hea - vy and
so drink drink drink and be I'll

Am7(+4)
Cmaj7(+6)
1.
deep to - night.
to - night.
2. I've
2.
D
F6
From the one you left be - hind
Bb6
G
D
from the one you left be - hind from the
F6
Bb6
G
(etc.)
one you left be - hind from the one you left be - hind.

SMITHS

PAINT A VULGAR PICTURE

At the record company meeting
On their hands – a dead star
and ooh, the plans that they weave
and ooh, the sickening greed
At the record company party
on their hands – a dead star
the sycophantic slags all say:
"I knew him first, and I knew him well"
Re-issue! Re-package! Re-package!
Re-evaluate the songs
double-pack with a photograph
Extra Track (and a tacky badge)
A-list, playlist
"Please them, please them!"
"Please them! please them!"
(sadly, THIS was your life)
but you could have said no
if you'd wanted to
you could have said no
if you'd wanted to
BPI, MTV, BBC
"Please them! Please them!"
(sadly, this was your life)
but you could have said no
if you'd wanted to
you could have walked away
. . . couldn't you?
I touched you at the soundcheck
you had no real way of knowing
in my heart I begged "please, take
me with you . . .
I don't care where you're going . . ."

But to you I was faceless
I was fawning, I was boring
just a child from those ugly new houses
who could never begin to know
who could never really know
Best of! Most of!
Satiate the need
slip them into different sleeves!
Buy both, and be deceived
climber – new entry, re-entry
World tour! ("media whore")
"Please the Press in Belgium!"
(THIS was your life . . .)
and when it fails to recoup?
Well, maybe:
You just haven't earned it yet, baby
I walked a pace behind you at the soundcheck
you're just the same as I am
what makes most people feel happy
leads us headlong into harm
so, in my bedroom in those 'ugly new houses'
I dance my legs down to the knees
but me and my 'true love'
we will never meet again . . .
At the record company meeting
on their hands – at last! – a dead star!
but they cannot taint you in my eyes
no, they cannot touch you now
No, they cannot hurt you my darling
they cannot touch you now
but me and my 'true love'
will never meet again

Paint A Vulgar Picture

Words by
MORRISSEY

Music by
JOHNNY MARR

Bm
G
A
G
A
the plans they weave and ooh
but you could have said no if you'd want - ed to you
but you could have said no if you'd want - ed to you
Bm
G
A
F♯
the sick - en - ing greed 2. At the
could have said no if you'd wanted to B. P. (to v. 4.)
could have walked a - way couldn't you.
B
E
F♯
B
re - cord com - pa - ny par - ty on their hands
5. I touched you at the sound check you had no real

E F♯ G♯m E F♯
a dead star the sy - cho - phan - tic slags all
way of know - ing in my heart I begged "take me
E G♯m E F♯
say "I knew him first and I new him well"
with you" "I don't care where you're go - ing
B E
re - is - sue re - pack - age re - pack -
but to you I was face - less I was fawn -
F♯ B E F♯
age re - e - val - u - ate the songs
ing I was bor - ing a child from those ug - ly new houses who could

VERSE *(As v. 1)* *(Instr.)*

VERSE: *(As v. 5)*

Best of! Most of! Satiate the need slip them into different sleeves!
Buy both and feel deceived climber new entry re-entry
World tour ("media whore") "Please the Press in Belgium"
(This was your life) and when it fails to recoup?
Well maybe:
You just haven't earned it yet baby.

VERSE: *(As v. 1)*

I walked a pace behind you at the soundcheck you're just the same as I am what makes most people feel happy leads us headlong into harm so in my bedroom in those 'ugly new houses' I dance my legs down to the knees but me and my 'true love' we will never meet again . . . .

VERSE: *(As v. 5)*

At the record company meeting on their hands at last! A dead star!
But they cannot taint you in my eyes no they cannot touch you now
No they cannot hurt you my darling they cannot touch you now
but me and my 'true love' will never meet again.

(FADE ON A7)

DEATH AT ONE'S ELBOW

Ooh Glenn
don't come to the house tonight
Ooh, Glenn
don't come to the house tonight
because there's somebody here
who really really loves you
stay home
be bored
(it's crap, I KNOW)
Ooh, Glenn
don't come to the house tonight
Ooh, Glenn
don't come to the house tonight
because there's somebody here
who'll take a hatchet to your ear
how the frustration renders me
hateful, Glenn!
don't come to the house tonight
don't come to the house tonight
because you'll slip on the
trail of my bespattered remains
and so, that's why
GOODBYE MY LOVE, GOODBYE MY LOVE
GOODBYE MY LOVE, GOODBYE MY LOVE
GOODBYE MY LOVE, GOODBYE MY LOVE
Belch

Death At One's Elbow

Words by
MORRISSEY

Music by
JOHNNY MARR

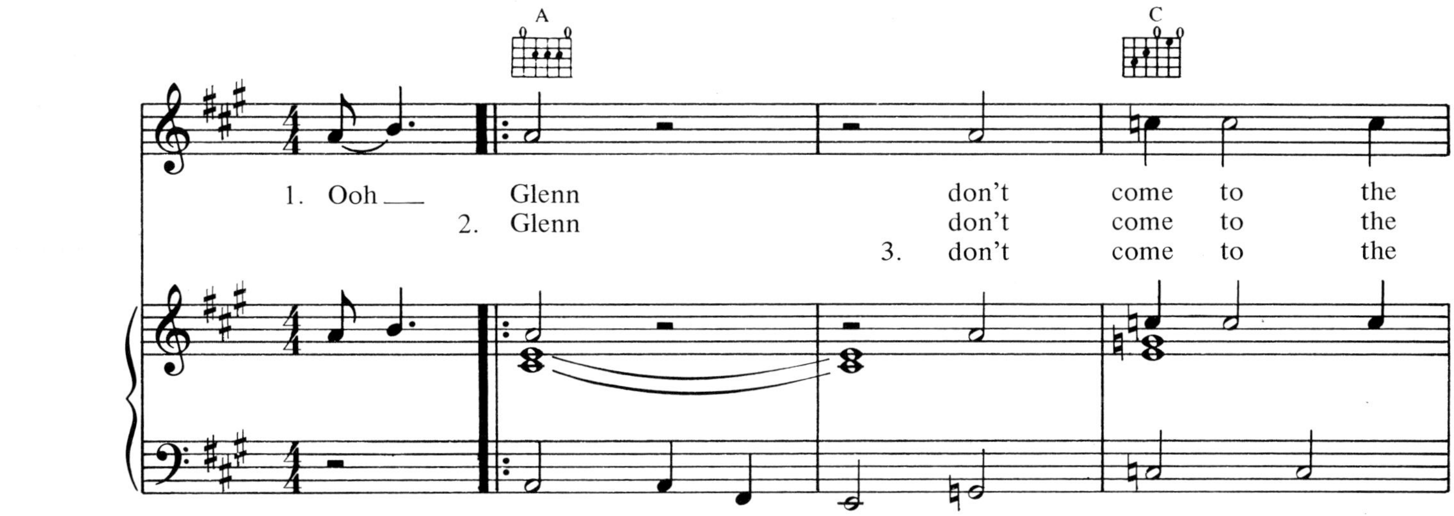

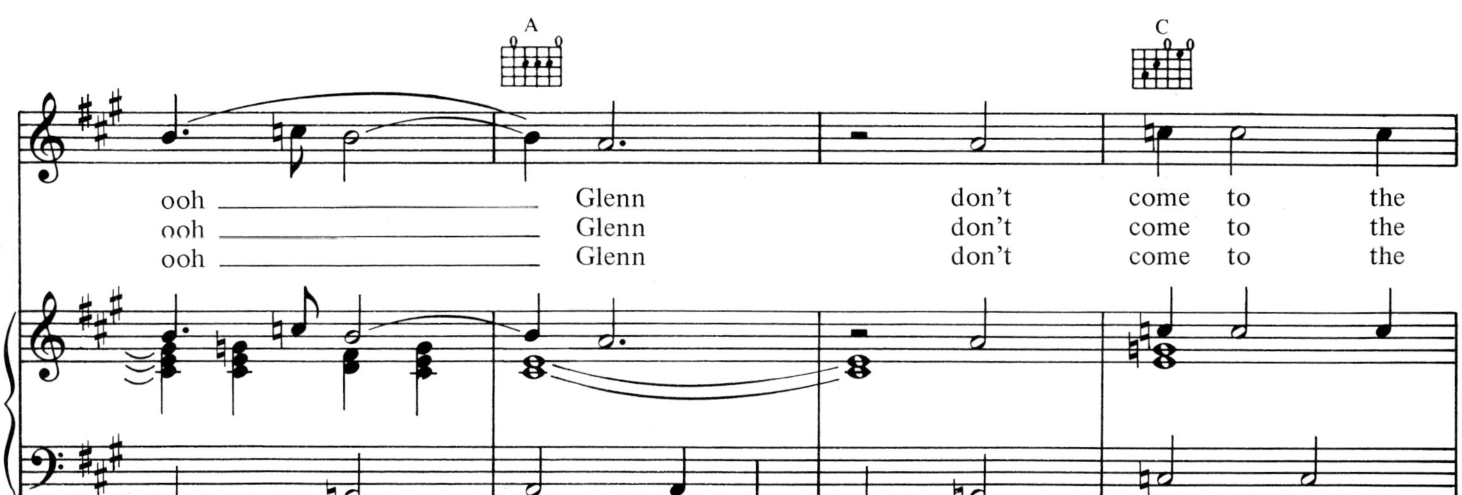

D
A7
house to - night.
house to - night.
house to - night.
Ooh Glenn
D7
be - cause there's some - bo - dy here who
be - cause there's some - bo - dy here who'll
be - cause you'll slip on the trail
A7
real - ly real - ly loves you ooh
take a hatchet to your ear
of all my sad remains that's

E
Glenn stay home be bored
the frus - tra - tion it ren -
why that's why good bye my love
F
G
it's crap I know to - night
ders me hate - ful Glenn!
good - bye my love good
1.
A7
ooh Glenn. Ooh

2.
A7
3.
E
F
G
bye my love good - bye my love.
A7
Good
E
F
G
A
bye my love good - bye my love.

45rpm
THE PRIMITIVES
stop killing me

I WON'T SHARE YOU

I won't share you
I won't share you
with the drive
the ambition
and the zeal I feel
this is my time
as the note I wrote
was read, she said
has the Perrier gone
straight to my head
or is life plainly sick and cruel, instead?
"YES!"
No – no – no – no – no – no
I won't share you
I won't share you
with the drive
and the dreams inside
this is my time
Life tends to come and go
well, that's OK
just as long as you know
Life tends to come and go
well, that's OK
just as long as you know
I won't share you
I won't share you
with the drive
and the dreams inside
this is my time
this is my time

I Won't Share You

Words by
MORRISSEY

Music by
JOHNNY MARR

G
Am
C
D7
time.
time.
time.
- - - ling.
The
Life
I want the
Bm
Em
note I wrote she read she said has the
tends to come and go
freedom and I want the guile I want the
C
D7
Per - ri - er gone straight to my head
that's O. K. as long as you know
free - dom and the guile oh

Bm
D7
or is life sick and cruel in -
life tends to come and go
life tends to come and go
Em
Em7
C
stead? "Yes" no no no no no no
as long as you know know know know know know
as long as you know know know know know know
D7
C
D
no no no no no no.
know know know know
know know know know

Printed in England
Panda Press · Haverhill · Suffolk • 11/87